Around
Wallingford

IN OLD PHOTOGRAPHS

High Street, Benson, *c.* 1912. On the right next to the Red Lion public house is Mr Harry West the builder's house. His children are standing at the front gate, one of whom is Olive West.

Around Wallingford

IN OLD PHOTOGRAPHS

DAVID BEASLEY

Alan Sutton Publishing Limited
Phoenix Mill · Far Thrupp · Stroud
Gloucestershire

First Published 1994

Copyright © David Beasley, 1994

Cover photograph: Lamb Corner. Bartlett's omnibus waits to take hotel guests to Wallingford railway station.

British Library Cataloguing in Publication Data.
A catalogue record for this book is available from the British Library.

ISBN 0–7509–0171–3

Typeset in 9/10 Sabon.
Typesetting and origination by
Alan Sutton Publishing Limited.
Printed in Great Britain by
Ebenezer Baylis, Worcester.

To the four ladies in my life: May Low my gentle grandmother, Jean Beasley my caring mother, Irene Leaver my thoughtful mother-in-law, Ann my loving wife.

Contents

High Street, Wallingford, 1935. All the buildings on the right-hand side of the road up to the centre of the photograph have been demolished.

Introduction

In Wallingford we are fortunate to have two very good sources of local history: the photographs and postcards of several local photographers, and the *Berks and Oxon Advertiser*, a newspaper printed in Wallingford between June 1855 and December 1941.

The most prolific photographer was James Alfred Latter, who came to Wallingford in the late 1880s. The family ran the business at 10 St Mary's Street for three generations; it was finally sold just short of its centenary year. James Latter was a keen cyclist and rode a tricycle around the district while taking photographs (the tricycle can be seen in some of his photographs). Latter's photographs are a considerable social document of late Victorian and Edwardian life recording most local events, from the Duke of York's wedding (George V) through to the Wallingford Territorials leaving for France in 1914 (an event in which one of his sons became a local hero). He published hundreds of postcards of Wallingford and district, which can be recognized by his terrible handwriting on the front of the card!

Latter was also a keen sportsman and was a shareholder in Southampton Football Club (his son William was goalkeeper for the club). Latter's was one of three shops in Wallingford that sold postcards, the others being Jenkins who were next door and Relf's in the High Street. Relf's shop was known as the postcard shop, although he didn't print his own but sold cards printed by firms like Frith & Co., Judges & Co., Frank Smith of Oxford and Warland Andrew of Abingdon, who rarely recorded the location of his excellent postcards. A. Jenkins published his own, but not of the same high quality that Latter did.

The second source, the *Berks and Oxon Advertiser*, was published by the Jenkins family. When the stamp duty on newspapers was repealed in 1885, Thomas Jenkins started the paper in June that same year, with his son William Daniel Jenkins on the editorial staff and financial backing from Henry Hawkins. Daniel took over the paper in 1861 and ran it until his death in 1921, aged eighty-one years.

The paper is a goldmine of local stories on all levels of the social scale. Through its pages you can meet the people from the Victorian and Edwardian eras, with stories ranging from parliamentary elections, when Wallingford had its own MP, to steam engines exceeding the 4 miles per hour speed limit in the Market Place. It also records the jubilee and coronation celebrations, as well as the terrible effects of the First World War in which the male population of Wallingford suffered a 20 per cent casualty rate. This paper is invaluable for any local historian wishing to learn about these periods of local history. In 1949 the paper was published again, but it was printed in Watlington and lost most of its local interest stories.

From these sources a very good picture can be drawn of what it was like to live in the Wallingford area between 1856 and 1941.

Jack Warner of *Dixon of Dock Green* fame being introduced to George Atkins, the projectionist at Wallingford Cinema, in 1952. Standing behind Jack Warner to the left is Mrs V. Jones. Behind George Atkins is Mr Drewitt, with Mr Warneford the manager on the extreme right.

SECTION ONE

Wallingford: the Town

Engraving of Wallingford Bridge, looking south, *c.* 1790, showing the old bridge, which was some 7 feet narrower than the present-day bridge. The bridge was widened in 1810 because of damage sustained the previous year. To the left can be seen the toll-house.

Rebuilding the central arches of Wallingford bridge, 1810, which collapsed during the flood of 1809. To the right can be seen the temporary wooden bridge used during reconstruction of the bridge. To the left is the arch of the bridge-chapel The Mary Grace.

The toll-house, built in 1819. In 1880 the gates were removed and the tolls ceased. The old toll collector, Mr Hearman, was allowed to live in the toll-house, and it continued as a private dwelling until 1934 when, despite protests, it was demolished. The bedrooms were at ground level and the living room at road level. The tricycle behind the toll-house belonged to Mr J.A. Latter, the photographer.

The north side of the bridge, photographed by Henry Taunt, 1885. On the far bank was the site of the old gasworks, which opened in 1835 despite the protests of the anti-illuminators. When the banks were damaged in 1874 the gasworks was closed and rebuilt next to the railway station. The Town Council converted the land into gardens, where concerts were held during the summer months.

Bossom's Wharf, c. 1908. Here barges from Oxford would unload their cargos. The gasworks was originally built alongside to allow the coal from the north of England to be unloaded directly into the works. Between the wars the wharf was used as a timber yard by Phillips of Crowmarsh.

Bridge House, *c.* 1880, when the house was occupied by a William Davis. Between 1842 and 1866 the house was owned by the Morrell family. In 1904 the house was purchased by Colonel Roberts of the 93rd Highlanders. During the Afghan War (1878–80) he took part in that epic march from Kabul to Khandahar. Col. Roberts was heavily involved with the Boy Scout movement in Wallingford until his death in 1916.

Castle Priory, built by Judge William Blackstone, 1759. His grandson, William Seymour, inherited the house in 1830, two years before he was elected MP for Wallingford. In 1843 Blackstone sold the estate to Thomas Duffield and to Howbery Park. In the 1860s a Miss Large ran a boarding school here. James Hayller RA (1828–1920) purchased the property in the mid–1870s. He and his family were well known in the art world.

Riverside, Thames Street. This was the home of George Dunlop Leslie RA (1836–1921) from 1882 to 1906. Many of his pictures were exhibited by the Royal Academy. The backdrop of the stage in the Free Library, a conception of Wallingford bridge in 1450, was painted by him.

Lower Wharf. This boating and swimming area, with the Wallingford and District Rifle Club building to the right of picture, was run by Percy Turner. Mr Turner was well known for singing comic songs at concerts held in the Rifle Club building. In 1910 the club moved to new premises in St John's Road. St Lucians, the large house behind the trees, was owned between 1860 and 1878 by the Hilliard family, when it was known as Wharf House. Richard Wilder purchased the house in 1878. He moved in 1887 and renamed the house St Lucians.

Chalmore Lock, *c*. 1870. Established in 1838 the lock was finally removed in 1883. It was known as a summer or low-water lock and weir, and was used to raise the water level in the summer months. The first lock-keeper was Stephen Wheeler, who was paid 12*s* a week; the toll was 2*d* per ton. The last lock-keeper was Charles Phillis.

High Street, *c*. 1908. On the extreme right is George Dell's cycle shop, while on the left, on the corner of Thames Street, is Morris's china and glassware shop. Calleva House, the tall building on the left, was built during the reign of George I for William Hucks, the MP for Wallingford. In 1888 it became a private school run by the principals Miss Bertha Payne and Miss F. Payne, who originally started the school on the corner of Castle Street opposite the Lamb Hotel.

High Street, further west, *c*. 1908. On the left is George Relf's stationers and postcard shop, which was also the servants' Registry Office. Next door was the office for the *Reading Mercury* and Registry Office, owned by Charles Venimore. The building with the flags flying is Tombs Temperance Hotel. On the right are the watchmaker William Beisley, the National Telephone Co. (where the lady with the white apron stands), Thomas Gibbons's shop (next door), followed by the International Tea Co. stores.

High Street, further west, *c.* 1924. On the left is Emery's tobacconist and hairdresser's shop, followed by the London Meat Co. on one corner of Wood Street. Opposite is A. Honeybone's saddle and harnessmaker's shop, with Ben Crudgington's fishmonger's next door. Behind the two ladies on the right is the Misses Gardener's sweetshop, Mr C.A. Evans was the proprietor of the George Hotel. Next door (out of view) is P. Carstairs wine merchants, while the Lamb Hotel, run by Mr J. Cox, can be seen in the distance.

Lamb Corner, *c.* 1906. Rusher's china shop is on the right, with Elizabeth Woolbridge's saddle and harnessmaker's shop next door. On the corner of St Mary's Street is the Hope and Anchor public house, run by Mrs Marion Saunders. Walter Hunt, seed merchants, is on the opposite corner. On the left is the house once owned by Richard Deacon, who was petitioned by the Liberals for inducement during a town election. He was accused of allowing seven voters to stay overnight and giving them dinner and breakfast. On telling the judge he didn't know they were there, he was let off.

Upper High Street, *c.* 1904. G. Butcher's, a boot dealer, is the first shop on the right followed by Sarah Butcher's sweetshop. The Beehive public house, where Mrs Kate Titcombe was landlady, can be seen with the street lamp on its wall. George Bruce Clarke's grocer's shop is behind the little boy. Next door is the Red Lion where William Walters was the landlord. The wagon in the centre appears to be part of a fun-fair. Note also the man with the milk churn.

Lamb Corner, *c.* 1930. When St Martin's Street was widened in 1938, Rusher's china shop was demolished. During a Council meeting a town councillor stated that widening St Martin's Street was a waste of money because Wallingford bypass would soon be built. The bypass was eventually opened in 1993. In 1926 Hunt's seed merchants moved to the Castle Street corner.

Castle Street, looking towards Lamb Corner, *c.* 1912. The Lamb Hotel is viewed here from the side. In the Bailiff's Account Book of 1584 the Lamb is referred to under its original name, the Bell. It was changed to the Lamb some time during the seventeenth century. St Hilda's had their Masonic Lodge here around the turn of the century. It was also the headquarters for the Royal Berks 1st Volunteer Battalion.

Castle House, *c.* 1908. This was the home of the Hedges family for most of its existence. Built in the early 1840s for John Kirby Hedges, it was demolished in 1972.

High Street, looking east, *c.* 1910. Goldsmith's Lane is on right, while partly hidden by the trees is St Alban's Priory, once the home of the Dalzall family. The house on the left is St Mary's Priory, the home of Mr Rogerson.

Kine Croft, looking south, *c.* 1910. During the Victorian period the Kine Croft was used for cricket matches. Bonfires were lit here on Guy Fawke's night. During the Crimean War an effigy of the tsar was burnt, as was an effigy of the Pope in 1850.

Market Place, *c.* 1908. The Town Hall dates from 1670 and also housed the town gaol which was located on the site of the ladies' toilet. In 1856 a new gaol was built in St Mary's Street. The steps on the left of the building were built in 1933. In front of the Town Hall are a number of farm implements, which were displayed by Wilder's on the days the Corn Exchange was open. The clock in St Mary's Church tower, which was installed by George Christie in 1869, replaced a diamond-shaped one. It was illuminated by three gas lights.

St Martin's Street, *c.* 1910. The two buildings on the right were demolished in 1936 to make way for the new post office. The building next to Church Lane used to be an alehouse called the Mermaid, which closed in 1876; the Lovelock family were landlords from 1779 to 1876. On the opposite corner of Church Lane was the Eight Bells (the name may be associated with the church bells). In the 1880s and '90s the bellringers of St Mary's Church held their annual Christmas dinners here.

Wallingford. St Mary's Street. up.

St Mary's Street, *c.* 1908. The large shop on the left is Pettits, established in 1856 when Thomas Pettit bought the property from Hatton and Rose. When built in the early 1850s, the site was known as New Buildings. Mr Shrimpton, the original owner, was an aggressive nonconformist who eventually became a clergyman. Next to Pettits is the police station, built by Moses Winter in 1856. On the right is the Primitive Chapel, which was built in 1890 on the site of the old Dukes Head which was pulled down in 1880. The vacant lot was used for prayer meetings until the chapel was built.

St Mary's Street, *c.* 1914. George Dell's garage was opened in 1911. Next door is the Farrier's Arms; the landlord at this time was Dennis Andrews. This beerhouse had two previous names: the King William IV and the Railway Arms. It was closed in 1909. In 1867 a policeman was caught drinking here while on duty; he escaped a reprimand because he said he had a cold and needed the drink for medicinal reasons. Where the lady wearing a white apron is standing, is N.J. Chapman's, a furniture dealer. The white building further down on the right, on the corner of Hart Street, is the King's Arms, which was closed in 1920. Roland Reading was the landlord.

St Mary's Street, looking north into St Leonard's Square, c. 1906. On the left is Mrs Joseph Morris's shop, next door is Ernest Scudd's china and hardware shop. The shops opposite are Harold Ayre's grocer's and Charlie Durham's fish shop. Left centre is the Free Library, which opened in 1870 and closed in 1936. It also served as the town museum during the 1920s under the management of Mr R.R. Hutchinson.

Wallingford Mill, c. 1925. The road here was originally much narrower, being only wide enough for a single vehicle to pass. When the old wooden front to the mill was removed and replaced with brickwork, part of the frontage was given up to allow the road to be widened. It was on the corner of St John's Road opposite in 1869 that William Young was stabbed by James Durbridge in a fight over a prostitute named Pratt. Although severely wounded, Young did survive. The building next to the mill is the Royal Standard, which was opened around 1859 when James Cheney was landlord.

Wood Street, looking north close to the new road junction, *c.* 1910. Charles Spyer, carpenter and undertaker, started his business in 1884 and bought out Samuel Naish in 1905. Opposite was Franklin & Gale's cattle market, now a car park. In 1870 the cattle sales were removed from the Market Place to the new road site after much discussion, one group wanting the sales to remain in the Market Place, and a second to move them to the Kine Croft where they had been held in the 1830s and '40s. On the right-hand side are the post office stables as well as what looks like a knife grinder outside the Fat Ox in the distance.

Croft Road, once known as Lock Lane, looking north, *c.* 1912. The house on the right is Croft House, run as a school from 1882 until the early 1920s by the Snow family. Mrs Thersia Snow, a Belgian lady, started the school, and her daughters, Thersia and Maria, continued it until its closure.

Entrance to Wallingford railway station, *c.* 1935.

Wallingford railway station, looking north, *c*. 1919. Completed in 1886 it was intended to continue the line to link up with Watlington via Benson, taking some eighteen months to complete. A proposal to build the line in 1855 was abandoned because it was intended the line should pass through the town centre.

Wantage Road, looking west, *c*. 1912. The cottage homes, which are just out of sight on the right, were opened in 1900 and were managed by the board of guardians. The house of local butcher Mr Lester is the first on the left. The terraced houses next to it were built in 1905.

SECTION TWO

Employment

Draper's shop in the Market Place, *c.* 1910. John Field first opened for business in 1808. Thomas Field, known by his staff as 'Governor Field', took over the business in 1843. By 1861 Henry Hawkins, who originally worked for Field as an assistant draper, had been made a full partner. Around 1885 Henry Ponking was offered a partnership. On market days a barrel of beer was kept under the counter and anyone making a purchase in the gentlemen's department was offered a drink. The business closed down in the 1920s. In the 1820s the left side of the shop was Wallingford post office, when Henry Stephenson was the postmaster.

The Oxford House Hotel, Market Place, *c.* 1900. Thomas Tappin, who is holding the horse, was the landlord. He came to Wallingford in 1893 with a reputation as a rick builder and prize-winning exhibitor with his rabbits and bantams, having previously worked as bailiff to Lord Dillon. The Oxford House was originally called the Queen's Head and was changed by W.B. Timms around 1862, possibly because he came from Oxford. The hotel was finally closed in 1907. Today it is Adkins estate agents.

Upton & Reynolds, chemists in St Mary's Street, 1906. Upton formed his partnership with Reynolds in 1895. When Upton died in 1897, Reynolds continued the business on his own until 1920 when he took Mr Johnson into partnership.

An 1890 advert for the Eight Bells public house, opposite St Mary's Church, on the corner of Church Lane.

Thomas Wheeler, grocery shop, *c.* 1908. Wheeler purchased the shop in 1895 from Payne & Keer. He was known for his wide range of blended teas and his selection of cheeses. In 1900 his China tea sold for 1*s* 10*d* for a 1 lb tin. The shop was situated next to the Corn Exchange in the Market Place and is now Lloyds Bank.

The International Tea Company in the High Street, *c.* 1912. The new shop-front was built in 1911. It is now part of the George Hotel and Wallingford sports shop.

Alfred Crudgington's fish and poultry shop in the High Street, *c.* 1920. Crudgington purchased the shop from Leech the butchers in 1919. Traffic pollution was not a concern to fishmongers in those days.

Tom Lester's butcher's shop, *c.* 1920. Lester's was the butcher in Wallingford for over 150 years. The little boy in the picture is Don Lester, whose father owned the business.

George Dell's cycle shop in the High Street next to the Town Arms, *c.* 1910. In 1911 Mr Dell opened a garage in St Mary's Street next to the present arcade. In 1913 the price for a Ford Runabout was £135; an extra £1 would be charged for a two-seater Dickey seat in the back. A Swift cycle in 1905 would cost £6 15s.

An advert for Murphy radios displayed behind John Hoddinot's electrical shop (the one lit up) in the High Street, 1936. John Hoddinot first moved to Wallingford in 1934; in the mid-1940s he moved to St Mary's Street where the fruit shop is now; and later he moved to St Martin's Street near the King's Arms. Hoddinot was the first to sell televisions in Wallingford. At the Corn Exchange in 1938 he gave a public demonstration of television.

The Fat Ox beerhouse on the corner of Hart Street and Wood Street in 1932. It was considered to be a very rough pub. In the backyard was a doss house, where anyone who couldn't afford the price of a room slept 'on the line'. This meant a rope was strung across the room, the sleeper stood close to the rope, draped his arms over, and slept standing up. There was a bowling alley in the 1880s, and Italian organ grinders and men with dancing bears were known to frequent the pub. The people in the picture are Henry Beasley, the landlord's son, and his wife Dora with their daughter Florrie.

The interior of the Beehive public house, High Street, *c.* 1942. Between 1934 and 1947 the Beehive was managed for Usher's Brewery by Cecil Low, a darts player of some note (the cup in the picture is a darts trophy won by the Beehive darts team). It was converted to the Berrick Restaurant in the 1970s.

Wallingford post office was opened in 1893 and was situated on the right-hand side of what is now Boots the Chemist. The building was constructed by Brashers and Son, Wallingford's most prominent builder of the era. The offices were open from 7 a.m. to 10 p.m. each weekday, including Saturdays, and 8 a.m. to 10 a.m. on Sundays. George Christie ran the previous post office in St Martin's Street from 1876 to 1893 when he retired. Before that Thomas Jenkins ran the post office from his premises in St Mary's Street from 1857 to 1874. On the pavement outside the office were written the words 'Post Office' in red and blue bricks.

The staff of Wallingford post office photographed by J.A. Latter, 1900. Back row, second from the left, is Thomas Trinder, with Mr Peters and Thomas's brother Alfred to the right of him. Ernie Gardener is sixth from the left. Thomas Trinder was killed at Gallipoli in 1915, Alfred was killed in France in 1916 and Ernie Gardener was wounded in France. In the front row, second from the right, is Adeline Wilder.

Wallingford post office staff, 1928. Back row, left to right: -?-, -?-, Painter, -?-, Bird, Frank Emmett, -?-, Honey, -?-, -?-, Leaver, -?-, Rolls, Ayres. Middle row: Blackwood, -?-, Broadway, -?-, -?-, Wetherall Postmaster, Broadway, -?-, -?-. Front row: Bennet, Woodley, Knight, Connie, Rolls, Syms, Dawson.

The post office, which opened in December 1936, is one of the few built with the Edward VIII royal cypher above the public entrance. It was fitted with an Automatic Telephone Exchange and in 1936 there were almost 250 subscribers. The Post Office claimed that letters posted in London by 3 a.m. would be delivered in Wallingford first post the same day.

C.D. Beasley, a telegram boy for the post office, in 1934.

Wilder's ironfoundry in Goldsmith's Lane, built in 1869. To the left of the chimneys can be seen the bell that sounded the start and finish of work.

SECTION THREE

Education
and Illness

The National School at the north end of Castle Street. It was erected in 1828 and supported by subscription and school fees. Ninety boys and forty girls attended the school in 1854. During the 1850s Thomas Bottomley was master and his wife, Selina, mistress.

Kine Croft Girls' School, 1927. Back row, left to right: Gladys Brewerton, Kath Mills, Rose Hester, Gertie King, Edith Brewerton. Second row: Amy Goddard, Doris Benning, Margaret Watts, Ivy Sadler, Ethel Green, Margaret Bell, Eileen Hagbourne, Audrey Tappin, Olive Emmett. Third row: Cis Dearlove, Doris Giles, Molly Hobbs, Phyllis Sowerby, Phyllis Wells, Ivy Dixon, Phyllis Bolton, Marjorie Emmett. Front row: Freda White, Winnie Coombs, Lolly Berry, Nora Freeman, Cottage Homes' girl.

Second Year Infant Class at the Kine Croft School, 1946. Back row, left to right: -?-, -?-, -?-, -?-, M. Farmer, -?-, -?-, Heather ?. Second row: Martin Crosskey, Frankie Feast, Bobby Morris, Bernie Atkins, John Belcher, Derek Moore, Billy Batten, Tony Morris, David Beasley, -?-, Abbot, -?-. Third row: -?-, -?-, Jean Wright, -?-, -?-, -?-, -?-. Front row: Brian Tilly, Sammy Griffin, Peter Shayller, John Chedsey, Freddie Hoskins, Peter Eldridge, Dickie Palmer, Burnham, Peter Buckle, Michael Whale, Dougie Sheard.

Council School, St John's Road, *c.* 1912. The school was opened on 5 April 1910. Brasher and Sons built the school and it was designed to accommodate 260 boys. While excavating the foundations, workmen unearthed a human skeleton of a man over 6 feet tall. But during the absence of the workmen, children broke up the remains.

The woodwork class at the Council School, *c.* 1912. The best examples of their work can be seen on the bench in the foreground.

The Cottage Hospital or Morrell's Memorial Hospital in Reading Road, *c.* 1908. The hospital was built in 1881 on land given by Henry Hawkins. Herbert Morrell donated £1,000 towards the cost of the building, which was done by William Brasher for £980 11*s*. In 1930 it was converted to a police station. It was demolished in the 1960s.

The Isolation Hospital, *c.* 1912. This was built in 1904 despite considerable public opposition because of the cost (it was thought a portable canvas hospital similar to one that was used at Thame would be good enough). In 1945 the author spent three months in the hospital with scarlet fever and was the only patient during that time.

The world famous opera singer, Dame Clara Butt, opening the Wallingford and District Hospital in July 1929. Her husband Mr Rumford is on her left.

The Wallingford Cottage Hospital, *c.* 1950.

Military Service

The Berkshire Yeomanry marching through Wallingford Market Place, September 1905. They were on their way to Newnham Murren, where they camped in a field called the Hundred Acres. They formed part of a large-scale manoeuvre to oppose an invasion of southern England by a European power.

Members of the 11th Berks (Wallingford) Rifle Volunteers at summer camp at Cookham, 1863.

4th Battalion Royal Berks at the Drill Hall in Thames Street, 1936. Back row, left to right: Westbrook, Allan, Fred Lovegrove, H. Frewn, Jim Brant, J. Hester, -?-, -?-, Goodenough, -?-, B. Brown. Second row: -?-, -?-, Sid Hobbs, -?-, B. Buckle, -?-, Snowy Whichlowe, Charlie Tame, 'Basher' Beasley, -?-, Herman, H. Bill, Tubb, Jack Laker. Front row: Griffin, G. Strudwick, A. Atkins, Barlow, B. Field, D. Gale, -?-, F. Summers, Harry Edwards, Freddie Spooner, -?-.

The Royal Berkshire Regiment at summer camp, *c*. 1910.

Contingent of B Company, 4th Royal Berks Regiment, at summer camp at Levant, Chichester, Sussex, August 1939. Back row, left to right: Bill Soden, George Strudwick, Syd Wernham, Charlie Soden, Frank Hobbs, Harry Grant, Bert Butcher, Vic Moffat, John Atwell, Len Davis. Centre: Clarence Rush. Front row: Harry Turner, Percy Rouse, Jim Douglas, Ted Goodall, Doug Sadler, Wilf Butcher.

Cavalry resting in Wallingford Market Place during the 1905 manoeuvres. The camp at Newnham Murren was open to the public on Sunday, and several thousand were thought to have visited during the day. Various regimental bands played throughout the day. This card is one of a set of twenty-five taken by local photographer J.A. Latter.

The Territorials leaving Wallingford in the middle of a thunderstorm, 13 August 1914. Wallingford, who formed a half company of the 4th Battalion Royal Berkshire Regiment, were billeted in empty houses near Swindon. A Wallingford man in a letter home complained that all the Swindon pubs were out of bounds to them.

Wallingford men who were repatriated from prisoner-of-war camps in Germany in 1919.

Red Cross nurses from the Wallingford area, *c.* 1917.

Henry Beasley, the last landlord of the Fat Ox, photographed during the First World War. Henry served with the 3rd Hussars in the Sudanese campaign of 1898 under Kitchener, and throughout the Boer War. After being discharged from the Army in 1902, he went goldmining with his brother in Canada. After six years he returned to England to marry, only to be called up in 1914. He served through to 1918 in the Royal Army Service Corps.

Eddie Latter, the son of J.A. Latter, the Wallingford photographer, c. 1918. When war broke out in 1914, Eddie Latter was in Canada and, with his friend Jenkins, immediately joined a Canadian regiment. In 1916 he was awarded the Military Cross for rescuing three wounded men while under continuous fire. By the end of the war he had been promoted to captain. During the influenza epidemic of 1918, he contracted the virus and died.

Peace celebrations in St John's Road, July 1919. Back row, left to right: W. Shuard, Elsie Pyke, Mrs W. Hobbs (jun.), Mrs Strange, G. Sadler, Mrs Pyke, Mrs Frances, Bingy Humphries. Front row: Mrs Sadler, Mrs Herbert, Mrs Hobbs (sen.), Nellie Fletcher, Mrs C. Blissett, Mrs Beal, Mrs W. Blissett.

Fancy dress party at the peace celebrations. Alfred Perry won first prize in the decorated perambulators' class. His mother is the lady on the right, standing next to Mr Newin who was dressed as John Bull. Alf Perry was for many years postman at Benson.

Wallingford Territorials marching along Wood Street, 1936. The sergeant leading is Bert Field. Front rank, left to right: -?-, Dickie Palmer, C.D. Beasley, Fred Summers.

SECTION FIVE
Relaxation

A dance in the Town Hall, *c.* 1927.

Wallingford Bridge on the coronation of George V, 1911. The decorations for the bridge were designed by Mr Turrill and Mr T. Clifton. Because of high winds the display wasn't seen at its best.

Queen Victoria's diamond jubilee, June 1897. The Market Place, photographed looking towards Dr Walter's house (now Barclays Bank), was decorated in red, white and blue flags, as well as a few stars and stripes. Payne's the jewellers (on the left) was decorated with Japanese lanterns.

Sports Day in the Kine Croft, jubilee day, 1897. The under-15 girls 100 yards final is taking place; the winner was Rose Bartlett, Emily Luckett was second and Kate Gunning third. The minor places were filled by Jessie Wheeler and Mary Hobbs.

Edward VII's proclamation, 1901. The proclamation was read by the mayor (Councillor Thomas Pettit), attended by Mr F.E. Hedges the town clerk, and the mace-bearer Mr W. Blackwood.

Edward VII's coronation preparations, 1902. The coronation was postponed from June because of the king's illness. Mr S. Nash was responsible for decorating the Town Hall. Some of the features of the day included the illumination of the town, a regatta, a water carnival, and a firework display.

Wallingford gymkhana, June 1908. The gymkhana was held at the Paddock, Reading Road, and was attended by over a thousand people. Here Miss Brown, nanny to Mrs F.K. Weedon, wins the decorated mail cart competition. Miss Collar, Dr Walter's nanny, was placed second.

The push-ball competition at the same gymkhana was won by Dorchester. The members were: J. Woods, P. Green, G. Gooding, A. Kirby, H. Brown, H. Winterborne, J. Greenaway and F. Chambers.

Musical chairs at the gymkhana, 1908. The game was won by A. Jenkins with W. Vokins runner-up.

The final of the pillow fight at the gymkhana, 1908. H.L. Chamberlain beat D. Taylor. Other winners were W. Crook in the costume race, W.J. Latter in the apple and bucket race, and Miss W. Peck in the telegram race.

Percy Turner's twins at Lower Wharf, *c.* 1907. The twins became famous for a short time in 1905 when their photograph appeared in an advert for baby food in several London illustrated newspapers. The advert also appeared in Chicago newspapers.

Skiff Regatta, 1907. The tug of war in punts was won by the Nondescripts, crewed by J. Snow, W.D. Jenkins (jun.), H. Hill, A. Jenkins, W. Goodenough, and H. Carling.

Skiff Regatta, 1907.

Revd Stewart Dyer in St Leonard's Lane, *c.* 1908. Sayer Milward Terrace, built in 1868, was named after the Revd Sayer Milward of St Leonard's Church.

The children of Francis Hedges of Castle House on holiday with their nanny. Left to right: John, Pamela, Diana, Rosemary, and a friend.

Wallingford Carnival, Wednesday 9 July 1930. This is the Class 1 winner, Pettits, passing along St John's Road. Second prize was won by Field, Hawkins and Ponkings, depicting John Field dress of 1808, the year they started trading.

The winner of the decorated private vehicle, Messrs Pettits, at the carnival, 1930. Mr Burton of Pettits took second prize, with Messrs A. Dunsdon and Keith Jenkins.

Four ladies showing the smartness of the Eugene Wave hair-style at the 1930 carnival.

The carnival passing from St Mary's Street into the Market Place, 1930. The parade started in the Kine Croft, where judging took place by T.E. Wells (the mayor), Mrs F.R. Hedges, Miss Diana Patrick, and Colonel J.R. Wyndham of St John House.

A fête in the castle grounds, 1924.

Celebrations for George VI's coronation held in the Bull Croft, 1937. Left to right: Ethel Rush (Mrs Davis), Olive Emmett (Mrs Robinson) and Marjorie Emmett (Mrs Constable).

George VI's coronation, 1937. The Wallingford Territorials fancy-dress entry. Back row, left to right: George Strudwick, -?-, -?-, Freddie Spooner. Front row: C. Beasley. -?-, Sidney Hobbs.

The coronation of Queen Elizabeth II, June 1953. Photographed outside the Row Barge in St Leonard's Lane are, front to back, left side: Jeff Blissett, D. Beasley, Martin Howes, 'Butch' Hughes, -?-, Vera Jones, J. Hockley, ? Hockley, -?-, -?-. Right side: Pete Robinson, Ann Robinson, -?-, Kathleen Ayres, Mike Turner, -?-, Rex Munday, Peter Wells, Marion Hughes. Standing, left to right: Jean Beasley holding Wendy Beasley, Bess Robbins, Mrs Hitchin, Mrs Hughes, Mrs May Low, Mrs Ayres, -?-.

Wilder's staff trip to Clifton Hampden, 1940. Among those present are: C. Gard, P. Attril, C. Tidmarsh, J. Hermon, D. Tidmarsh, T. Bond, Albert, Aldridge, A. Horn, J. James, G. Crook, R. Stevens, Joe Eversden, R. Marks, E. Capel, J. Harmer, J. Crook, R. Crook, G. Becket, E. Flowers, S. Honey, -?-, J. Collins, J. Wilder, Mr Gard (sen.), G. Thomas, Mr Sparks, F. Busby, J. Thomas, R. Keeps, C. Hermon, D. McDonald, A. Baber, G. Thomas, H. Wilder, R. Harris, A. Thomas, L. Walters, Miss Wilder, B. Goodenough, D. Wilder, Brooker, A. Honeybone, T. Wilder, F. Chedzey, B. Doe, B. Neighbour, C. Tyler, J. Saunders, C. Dumper, F. Spooner, L. Baber, S. Frewin, T. Capel, G. Griffin, J. Clinkard.

Freddie Snow at an archaeology excavation in his scrapyard next to St John's School, 1937. The skeleton is of an Anglo-Saxon princess and was the tenth skeleton found in the scrapyard in the 1930s. The skeleton was aged about twenty and suffered with curvature of the spine. The scrapyard was the site of the Wallingford Rifle Club and the Pavilion. The latter opened in 1910 and was used for dances and other functions.

Howbery Park Hockey Club, 1909. The club, which had its pitch in the grounds of Howbery Park, was founded in 1903. Mr Harvey du Cros, the owner of Howbery Park, was president. Some of the players photographed here include Mr Curtis, V. Hughes, H. Tustin, F.K. Weedon, C.C. Angel, P. Ponking, G. Jenkins, Miss Dyer, Miss Franklin.

Wallingford Hockey Club, c. 1928. The club was founded in 1894. The lady fifth from the right is Miss F. Nash, schoolmistress at St John's School for many years.

The projection room of Wallingford Regal Cinema, *c.* 1952. The film canisters on the projectors ran for twenty minutes; they took almost twenty minutes to change, so the projectionists had little time to rest during a three-hour performance.

The Regal Cinema, 1954. The cinema was opened in March 1934 by Major Harold Lovelock. The building was designed by Captain H. Cox to give the same comfort as a London super cinema.

WALLINGFORD'S LUXURY CINEMA

THE

REGAL

Opening Saturday, March 17th at 2.30 p.m.

And Continuing Monday, Tuesday and
Wednesday, March 19th, 20th and 21st
with
Bebe Daniels and Clifford Mollison in

"A SOUTHERN MAID"

Thursday, Friday and Saturday, March 22nd, 23rd and 24th

"DINNER AT 8"

With the Banquet of the Stars—
Marie Dressler, John and Lionel Barrymore
Wallace Beery and Jean Harlow, etc.

Sunday, March 18th

Douglas Fairbanks in

"ROUND THE WORLD IN NINETY MINUTES"

Prices of Admission 1 6 1/- and 7d.
(Including Tax).
Children under 14 years accompanied by Adults
7d. and 9d.

Continuous Mondays, Tuesdays, Wednesdays,
Thursdays and Fridays.
Three Separate Performances Daily on
Saturdays and Bank Holidays.
Sundays at 7.45
Matinee Wednesday and Saturday.
FREE CAR PARKING.

The advert for the first performance at the Regal Cinema, March 1934.

Wallingford Boy Scouts at camp on the Isle of Wight, 1955. Back row, left to right: Martin Whillock, Gardener, Frankie Feast, Basher Beasley (Scoutmaster), Brian Rush, D. Beasley, Martin Crosskey. Front row: John Jeskins, Andrews, David Nunn.

SECTION SIX

Floods and Snow

Floods in Winterbrook, 1894. Despite the flooding, the post was still delivered, with the postmen passing the mail upto the bedroom windows.

The 1904 flood before it reached its peak, photographed by A.J. Latter. Note there are no steps from the bridge roadway to the river bank; these weren't built until 1909.

Bill Goodenough, known as 'Old Bill', was boatman at Percy Turner's boathouse near the bridge for fifty years. The maintenance of Dame Clara Butt's boats was his special responsibility. During the June flood of 1903 Old Bill won a bet by punting his punt through the front doors of the Town Arms and ordering a pint. He is seen here in the uniform of a Special Constable in which he served for nearly fifty years.

Wallingford bridge during the 1947 flood. The boy looking over the steps parapet is Peter Baber, the lady standing by the bridge street light is Mrs Cope who is pregnant. The daughter she subsequently had, Valerie, married Peter Baber.

The great snowstorm, 26 April 1908. In twenty-four hours 20 inches of snow fell paralyzing the south of England. The seven o'clock Sunday postal delivery was not delivered until past three o'clock in the afternoon. Train services were severely delayed or stopped altogether.

Wallingford bridge after the severe snowstorm, 1908. The thaw was rapid and, combined with heavy rain, caused serious flooding in the Thames Valley. The Thames at Wallingford rose 31 inches in twenty-four hours. This and the previous picture were taken by A.J. Latter.

Crowmarsh

The Street, Crowmarsh, looking west toward Wallingford, *c.* 1904. On the right is the Bell Inn, where the beer was supplied by Shillingford Brewery. Opposite is the Old Reading Road. This road originally lined up with Lane End, but when Newnham Manor was enlarged in 1862 the road was realigned to its present position.

The Street, looking west, *c*. 1910. Newnham Cottage, first on the left, was built in 1908 and occupied by the Woodley family for many years. The Queens Head is in front of the trees on the left. Note Latter's tricycle by the side of the road.

Benson Lane, looking south, *c*. 1912. The old National School built in 1844 by William Blackstone is on the right. In 1850 it was united with the National Society. When a new Elementary School was opened opposite in September 1908, it was used as an infants' school. Worn into the brickwork of the school are a large number of grooves; these were formed by schoolchildren sharpening their slate pencils by rubbing them on the walls.

Crowmarsh Elementary School, *c.* 1927. Back row, left to right: Joey Cairns, George Atkins, Phillip Higgs, Ernie Harvey, Lewis Berry, Jim Higgs, -?-, Cyril Heathcote, Stanley Wallin, Jimmy Gifford. Centre row: Billy Frewin, Joan Evans, -?-, -?-, Gwen Bowden, Rachel Frewin, Ivy Alder, Beryl Varney, Joy Brown, Phyllis Jessop, Kathy Bird, -?-, Jessie Skidmore. Front row: Miss Chapman, George Higgs, Mary Frewin, Margaret Frewin, Peter Smith, Ken Smith, Fred Beesley, Queenie Rollings, Don Dearlove, Ruby Dearlove, Mary Honey, Lily Pummel, Tommy Pummel, Fred Harvey, Mrs Rathbone.

Crowmarsh Home Guard in the playground of Crowmarsh School, *c.* 1942. The third man from the left in the back row is Joe Lay, next to him is Sid Painting. In the centre row, first from the left, is Reg Lovegrove, eighth from the left is Wilder, next to him is Amos Frewin, Harvey. Second from the left in the front row is Wheeler, fifth is Bill Green.

Benson Lane, *c.* 1908. To the left are the grounds of Howbery Park. In 1908 the Howbery estate was owned by Harvey du Cros.

Howbery Manor-House, *c.* 1908. The house was designed by Hakewell and although started in 1833 it wasn't finished until 1854. Williams-Wynn bought the house in 1867 from Alfred de Morney. Wynn died in 1895, and after several years on the market Harvey du Cros purchased the estate. When du Cros died in 1918 Lord Wittenham purchased the estate.

The Stables Howbery

Gardeners' and engineers' cottages, *c.* 1910. These were built in 1885 by Williams-Wynn on the site of seventeenth-century stabling. The building on the left was built on the site of a gasometer, which provided heat and light to the estate.

Williams-Wynn's coach in the grounds of Howbery Park. The groom holding the horse's head is Mr Wheeler.

Crowmarsh village, looking east, *c. 1925*. The building on the left is the Limes, which was built in the eighteenth century and demolished in 1976. Next door is Dearlove's bakery and post office. The Gardener's Arms is the white building next to the lorry. Mr Wise, who lived in the house next to the one with the creeper, was a part-time undertaker. Each night he would take his horse through the living-room to the backgarden.

Wallingford Church choir's family outing, *c. 1912*. Dennis Andrews, possibly the man driving the first cart, was landlord of the Greyhound public house in St John's Road.

Heavy flooding caused by rapidly melting snow running down from Crowmarsh Hill, 1940. The stream that once ran down one side of the road was unable to cope with such a heavy flow of water.

Wilder's ironfoundry, c. 1920. The foundry was started in 1868 by Leonard Wilder on the site of Howbery Farm. When Leonard died in 1887 the business was taken over by his son Walter Wilder.

Walter Wilder in the grounds of his foundry *c.* 1920. Part of the old farm buildings can be seen in the background. Walter was well known as a singer; he and his family often sang at local concerts.

Ice House Hill, near the new Mongewell roundabout on the road to Reading, *c*. 1912.
The hill is named after an ice house built in 1783 to supply Mongewell House with ice.

SECTION EIGHT
Mongewell

Mongewell House, *c.* 1876. The Fraser family lived here for many years and finally bought the house and land in 1888. When Mr and Mrs E. Fraser celebrated their golden wedding anniversary in 1883, they invited the Town Council to a dinner and firework display at Mongewell. The councillors were taken to Mongewell by boat, with the bridge and river banks illuminated by Chinese lanterns.

St John's Church, photographed by H. Taunt *c.* 1876. The bell tower was built in 1791, when the church was renovated by Shute Barrington.

Mongewell House, *c.* 1910. The house was built in 1889 for Alexander Fraser downstream from the original house. When Fraser died in 1916 the house was used as a hospital for officers during the rest of the war. Howard Gould, the American millionaire, purchased the house in 1918. During the Second World War it was used as a convalescent home for the RAF. In 1953 it was purchased and converted to Carmel College.

Mongewell and North Stoke School, *c.* 1908. This opened in 1903 and replaced the old Estate School. When the Estate School closed, one of the pupils, Rosie Hilton, presented the schoolmistress Miss Wilder with a large family Bible.

The headmistress of Mongewell and North Stoke School riding her Enfield motor cycle, *c.* 1926. Her son and daughter are riding pillion.

Country dancing at Mongewell School, *c.* 1925. Because Dame Clara was interested in folk dancing, she paid for the mistress to go to various folk dancing classes, and she in turn passed what she learnt on to the children.

Empire Day, 24 May, at Mongewell School, *c.* 1925. The children sang Elgar's 'Land of Hope and Glory' instead of the national anthem because Dame Clara Butt, who was famous for singing Elgar's song, lived in the village.

Mongewell Farm, *c.* 1945. Teddy Townsend was leasing the farm at this time.

Harvest-time at Mongewell Farm, *c.* 1945.

An aircraft which landed in a field between Mongewell and North Stoke, *c.* 1926. In 1934 Mr Frost opened Wallingford Aerodrome at the top of Crowmarsh Hill near Oakley Wood.

SECTION NINE

Ipsden

St Mary's Church, Ipsden, *c*. 1907. Each year the choir of Ipsden Church was given an outing, paid for by Mr Arding of Braziers Park.

Interior of St Mary's, Ipsden, c. 1906. In 1890 Mr Arding paid for the choir to see the military exhibition in London. On their return he gave them supper at Braziers Park. Mr and Mrs Arding both accompanied the choir for the whole day.

Ipsden village, c. 1908. The building that can be seen in the distance down the road is where Wilder's of Wallingford first started its ironfoundry business.

Ipsden post office, *c.* 1910. The post office was run by Miss Janet Lindsey for many years. Miss Lindsey can be seen sitting on the fence.

Ipsden School, *c.* 1909. Miss Hannah Wear was schoolmistress at this time and may well be the lady standing by the doorway. The school was enlarged in 1897, when a room for infants was added. In 1854 the school had thirty pupils; Mr and Mrs Crews were headmaster and headmistress then.

Braziers Park, Ipsden. Although parts of the house were built in 1688, it was considerably enlarged by Isaac Manley between 1795 and 1799, with drawings of the house exhibited at the Royal Academy in 1799. Edward Wells, the Wallingford brewer, bought the house as a wedding present for his son Alfred Charles in 1880. When Alfred's uncle died, he was named in his will as the heir on condition that he changed his name to Arding. This he duly did in 1890.

Staff of Braziers Park, *c.* 1890. Arding was a great beneficiary to the villagers of Ipsden. He built a small hall in the grounds for the use of the community. Valentine Fleming of Nettlebed (related to Ian Fleming of James Bond fame) bought the house in 1906.

Chiltern Open-air Sanatorium, *c.* 1912. This convalescent home for people recovering from TB was run by Dr Charles Reinhardt.

Ipsden schoolchildren in front of the cricket pavilion, 1924.

SECTION TEN

North and South Stoke

Mill House, North Stoke, *c.* 1910. The mill was owned by the Clarke family for six generations, from the early eighteenth century into the twentieth century. Before the fence was put up, carters could take carts into the mill stream to allow their horses to drink and to soak their cart wheels.

Springs, North Stoke, *c*. 1910. Built in 1893 for Alexander Condie, the house was sold in 1902 to John Wormald. He extended the house in 1914, selling it in 1929. In 1919 he received a knighthood for services during the First World War.

Village Hall, North Stoke, *c*. 1914. The Village Hall was built in 1911 as a memorial to Edward VII by John Wormald. During the 1919 peace celebrations the weather was so wet that the festivities were held in the hall. Dame Clara Butt, the opera singer who lived in the village at Prospect House, sang at the celebrations.

North Stoke village, *c.* 1912.

South Stoke village and St Andrew's Church, *c.* 1906.

South Stoke Elementary School, which opened in 1877 for 110 children. In 1907, the
year this photograph was taken, Mr Lawrence Kirby was the schoolmaster.

South Stoke main street, looking north towards the church, *c.* 1910. The cottages on the
right were demolished in the 1960s. The white house in the centre is the Plough public
house.

The South Stoke fire, 1905. This was the third serious fire in South Stoke in less than forty years. The first, in 1868, destroyed six cottages and farm buildings; in the second in 1873 two cottages and some farm buildings were destroyed. The third destroyed four cottages and several farm buildings.

Ferry Road, South Stoke, 1905. The chimney in the centre is all that remains of one of four cottages destroyed in the fire. The fire travelled along Ferry Road from Brock's Farm to College Farm and from there to Manor Farm.

The Leathern Bottle inn between South Stoke and Goring photographed by H. Taunt, 1876. In 1903 Mr T. Burns was the landlord.

Goring

Arthur Cocks' store, High Street, Goring, *c.* 1910. The shop on the left, where Mr Cocks ran his drapery business, was the old British School which opened in 1850. Mr Cocks' business was here from 1876 to 1915.

Saunder's boatyard, 1890s. The yard was situated just north of Streatley bridge. The owner of the boatyard, Mr S.E. Saunders, is about to embark on a river trip.

Nun's Acre, Goring, *c.* 1912. Between 1888 and 1895 the house was occupied by Percy Stone.

Cleeve Mill, located upstream between Streatley bridge and Cleeve Lock, *c.* 1912. In 1910 the lock-keeper was J. Willey, who won first prize for the best-kept lock garden. While serving in the Royal Navy during the First World War he was awarded the DSM. In 1919 he was found drowned in the river.

The approach to Streatley bridge, *c.* 1906. This bridge was built entirely of timber in 1837, with a toll-house on the Streatley side. The toll for a four-wheeled carriage was 3*d*, and for a carriage, propelled by anything other than animal power, 1*s*. This bridge was replaced by the present one in the 1920s.

The Miller of Mansfield, *c.* 1914. At this time Mrs N. Cooper was landlady. On the right is the chapel which was opened by William List in 1893.

Streatley Mill, *c.* 1914. There was a mill here in 1583. Unlike its neighbour at Goring, which was used as an electricity generating station, Streatley Mill was used until the 1920s when it was burnt down. It was near here in 1674 that an accident with the ferry boat resulted in sixty people drowning.

The Bull Hotel, Streatley, *c.* 1912. Mr Herbert Roberts was the landlord.

Goring and Streatley Regatta, looking north, 1912. One of a series photographed by Henry Taunt. The regatta ceased because of the First World War, but has recently been revived.

SECTION TWELVE
Moulsford

The Beatle and Wedge pub, Moulsford, c. 1890. The ferry to South Stoke departed from here. In January 1891 the weather was so cold that the river froze and people were able to walk across from South Stoke to Moulsford. The day after the fire at South Stoke in 1905, over a thousand people crossed from Moulsford to see the devastation caused to Manor Farm.

Moulsford Rifle Range and Village Hall, *c.* 1908. Rifle clubs became very popular after the Boer War. This was a contributory factor in the high standard of rifle fire attained by the Regular and Territorial Armies in the early days of the First World War.

The Grange, Moulsford, *c.* 1910.

The main road through Moulsford, *c.* 1906. On the extreme right is the village school.

Moulsford post office and village shop, *c.* 1935.

Moulsford village, looking north, *c.* 1908. During the jubilee celebrations in 1897 the village was decorated with flags and bunting; in the evening each cottage illuminated their windows with candles. Moulsford, for some reason, celebrated the jubilee two weeks after the rest of the country.

St John's Church, Moulsford, photographed by Henry Taunt, 1876.

SECTION THIRTEEN
Cholsey

Little Stoke ferry, 1876. Mr Scott Jervis of Littlestoke twice erected a gate across Littlestoke Ferry Road. The first was removed by local people, the second time he was ordered to remove it by the courts. The Berkshire Asylum, which can be seen in the distance, was opened in 1869.

Cholsey railway station, looking west, c. 1905. The station replaced Moulsford Road station in 1892. Because the track was widened at the same time, the old brick roadbridge on the Reading Road was blown up and replaced with a temporary wooden structure until the iron bridge was built alongside. The demolition was witnessed by over two thousand people.

Station Road, Cholsey, c. 1910. When this road was being constructed, human remains were discovered. The bodies were thought to date back to the Civil War as no remains of coffins were found.

Honey Lane, Cholsey, *c.* 1912.

Sawyer's drapers and clothiers shop in Honey Lane, looking north, *c.* 1906. The horse and cart belonged to Hutt and Sons the coal merchants.

The Beehive public house, Honey Lane, *c*. 1908. Mr Mark Wells was the landlord. The Beehive was owned by the Hanley Brewery of Oxford.

The Green at Cholsey, known as The Forty, *c*. 1930. In 1810 a roundhouse was built here to be used as a lock-up. Robert Bosher, who had deserted from the Army, was locked up for the night, but friends in the village passed him a screwdriver through the bars and he managed to unscrew the lock and escape. The village constable had quite a shock in the morning when he came to check on him; he immediately arrested Robert's mother Sally. The local JP, Mr Joseph Arnould of Whitecross, released her after giving her breakfast.

The Old Cholsey post office, situated in the Wallingford Road, on the corner of Little Lane, photographed just before the First World War.

The Vicarage, Cholsey, *c*. 1909.

St Mary's Church, Cholsey, *c*. 1880. The building on the right is the old school. During the very hot summer of 1893 there was an outbreak of typhoid fever, and the school was used as a temporary isolation hospital.

Wallingford Road, Cholsey, *c*. 1910. In the distance can be seen the sign for the Red Lion public house.

Pantner's Road, Cholsey, photographed just after the houses were built, *c.* 1930.

Buckland House, Cholsey, *c.* 1914. Situated on the Reading Road Buckland House was the home of William Wright between 1864 and 1877. A rummage sale held here in 1893 raised £11 for sick children; 150 people attended.

The Nag's Head, Winterbrook, *c.* 1910. Mr Morris was the landlord. Just before the terraced houses on the right is the entrance to Mr Cato's nurseries.

SECTION FOURTEEN
Shillingford

Shillingford Bridge Hotel, formerly called the Old Swan Inn, *c.* 1908. The hotel was owned by several generations of the Reynolds family between 1849 and 1905. It had electricity for lighting in 1889.

Shillingford bridge, looking north, *c.* 1906. The old toll-house can be seen to the left of the bridge. In 1856 some two hundred horsemen pursued a stag across the bridge to Wittenham Clumps, where it was captured and later released.

The scene of an accident at Shillingford bridge, early 1930s. The man with his foot in plaster is the unlucky driver.

Shillingford bridge, when the river froze during the severe winter of 1940.

The Lodge at Shillingford Court, *c*. 1912.

Shillingford crossroads, *c.* 1935. Just out of sight to the right was the Old Bell public house, which was pulled down in 1965. Harold and Peggy Morris were the last managers.

The New Inn, Shillingford, *c.* 1912. The inn was located on the main Oxford Road. In 1894 flood-water reached a depth of 3 inches in the bar. Opposite is the George Inn, which closed in 1913.

Wharf Road, Shillingford, *c*. 1935. Mrs Wilson was the sub-mistress at the post office on the right.

Shillingford Court, *c*. 1912. Upstream from Shillingford bridge, this was built in the early 1900s, reputedly for Edward VII's favourite, Lily Langtry. The Haggie family lived there until 1916, when Mrs Haggie died.

Shillingford ironworks, *c.* 1895. When it closed down in 1899 over seventy men lost their jobs. It was originally Shillingford Brewery and was owned by Mr Field, the Wallingford draper, and Mr Thomas Payne of Shillingford.

Warborough

Warborough post office, *c.* 1912. Cycling became very popular during the Edwardian era. With the increase in wages, cycles became available to the working man. In 1900 a new cycle would cost £8, a secondhand one £2.

Maypole dancers in the grounds of Warborough Vicarage, *c.* 1905.

A Greet family wedding at St Lawrence, *c.* 1908. The boy standing by the rear wheel of the wedding coach is wearing clothes obviously handed down from an elder brother, allowing him room to grow.

George V's coronation, 1911. This photograph shows Mr Shrubb's barn, beside the village green, where dinner and tea were held for the villagers. The clergyman in the centre is the Revd Caldicott, vicar of Warborough.

Warborough Green, *c*. 1875. In 1899 the pavilion on the edge of the green was destroyed by fire. The fire engine was quickly on the scene but, despite this and the efforts of Messrs Langford, Bailey, Shrubb, Bond, Applebee and the Revd Caldicott, the pavilion was completely gutted.

Mr J.P. Holliday rethatching the roof of the Six Bells Inn, Warborough, *c.* 1930.

The Cricketer's Arms, *c.* 1907. It was near here in 1862 that Harry Frewin, Harry Archer and George Smith were charged with playing pitch and toss on a public highway. They each received a fine of 2*s* 6*d*.

Warborough Armistice Day parade, 1930s. Before the Second World War Armistice Day was always held on 11 November and everyone would stand for a minute's silence, no matter where they were or what they were doing.

The girls of Warborough School, *c.* 1895.

SECTION SIXTEEN

Dorchester

Dorchester High Street, looking north, *c.* 1908.

Dorchester High Street, looking south, *c.* 1910. The building on the left is the Missionary College of St Peter and St Paul. The college was opened on 30 October 1878; Revd Roberts was the principal.

High Street, Dorchester, *c.* 1906. The Crown Inn is on the right. Miss Emily Whichelo was the landlady at the time.

Lich-gate, Dorchester Abbey, *c.* 1912.

Dorchester Abbey, *c.* 1908.

The bridge at Dorchester, 26 April 1908. Workmen are clearing away some of the 20 inches of snow that fell in twenty-four hours.

Overy Mill, near Dorchester bridge, *c.* 1912. The mill was owned in 1907 by Mrs Fanny Turner.

Near Overy Mill, where nine bullocks were struck and killed by lightning, 9 August 1893. The carcasses were sold to Mr Passey of Oxford, who later moved to Benson and opened a slaughterhouse and scrapyard.

Day's Lock, *c.* 1914. The lock was built in 1788, although the first lock was built here in 1580. The tolls were 4*d* per ton. The footbridge in the background replaced the old swingbridge in 1870 at a cost of £250.

Aerial view of Dorchester, looking south, *c.* 1935.

Benson

Benson Church, *c.* 1910. During an attempt to enclose Benson parish in 1830 a notice announcing the enclosure was to be put on the church door. However, such a large crowd gathered around the church that the notice could not be put up. Unfortunately rioting ensued and a number of threshing machines were broken up on Mr Shrubb's and Mr Eyre's farms.

London Road, Benson, *c.* 1908. Now known as the Old London Road it was once the coach route through Benson to London, going straight across the airfield and linking up with the road at Beggar Bush Hill.

Brook Street, Benson, *c.* 1905. The Lamb and Flag public house is just behind the children on the right. In 1850 Benson had eleven licensed premises.

The Crown Inn, Benson, c. 1928. The Crown was an old coaching inn. At the turn of the century, as a tourist attraction, a four-horse coach ran between Oxford and London, breaking its journey at Benson.

High Street, Benson, c. 1908. The Free Church on the left was opened in 1879, but not with everyone's approval. In 1891 the Revd Simcox of Ewelme refused to marry Ann Franklin because she had attended a service at the Free Church.

Pengilly's store, High Street, Benson, *c*. 1928. Ronald Pengilly is the man standing in the doorway. Pengilly's also had a shop in Wallingford.

High Street, Benson, decorated for Edward VII's postponed coronation, August 1902. After tea, which was held at College Farm, F. Cook, J. West and Mrs W. Gurney won several prizes at the sports events.

Benson Coronation Festivities.

The Committee request the pleasure of the Company
of ......W. Frampton......
to Dinner at College Farm, Benson,
on Thursday, 26th inst., at 12 o'clock.

June 18th, 1902.

A. G. GRAY,
Hon. Sec.

Invitation card for a celebration dinner in honour of Edward VII's coronation, June 1902. Because of the king's illness the coronation was postponed until August. William Frampton lived at Hale Farm.

High Street, Benson, *c.* 1912. The Red Lion public house on the left was originally on the opposite side, on the corner of Mill Lane. Benson Mill, occupied by John Slade, was burnt down in 1890.

The Ship Inn, *c.* 1909. The inn was in the High Street opposite Mill Lane. Mr Jennings was the landlord in 1909; Mrs Jennings is possibly the lady standing in the doorway.

Castle Square, Benson, *c.* 1912.

Wood's stores, Castle Square, Benson, *c.* 1930. Left to right: Frank Harberr, John Woods, -?-, -?-, Mr Wood, the owner.

Benson Girl Guides camp in Dorset, 1930. Back row, left to right: -?-, Joan Pether, Ivy Painter, -?-, -?-, ? King-Edward, ? Ruck-Keene. Middle row, third from left: Alice Lane; fifth: Joan Walters. Front row, sixth from left: Ida Young; seventh: Dorothy Dutfield.

Queen Elizabeth's coronation, 1953. Back row, left to right: Jane Harkness, Jean Harber, Daphne Roberts, -?-, D. Spiers. Front row: Sandra Duncan, Penny Mornings, Richard Harber, Sue Roberts, Muriel Passey, Jackie Duncan, Janet Hutchins, Andrea Hutchins, -?-, Peter Passey, Bobbie Beal, Colin Keeble.

Benson School, mid-1940s. Back row, left to right: Teacher, Pat Aldridge, Barbara Cherrill, Pam Green, Mavis Town, June Dancer, Sylvia Woolridge. Third row: Joan Tulty, Ann Field, Maurice Haines, George Skinner, Tony Woodward, -?-, -?-, Brown, -?-. Second row: Rosemary Spiers, Bridget Salter, -?-, Nelly Wheeler, Amy Beal, Muriel Blizzard. Front row: -?-, -?-, -?-, John Webb, -?-.

Benson Social Club, on the corner of Crown Lane and Brook Street, 22 June 1910. It was opened on this day by Miss Ruck-Keene, the lady standing in the gateway.

The opening of St Helen's Avenue, mid-1930s. This was Benson's first bypass.

Benson Lock, photographed by Henry Taunt, *c.* 1876. The lock was built in 1870. The lock-keeper John Whiteman was paid 13*s* a week. Unfortunately in 1887 he was found drowned in the weir nearby, leaving a family of eight.

Swan Inn, Preston, Crowmarsh, 1947. The flood was the third highest recorded on this stretch of the Thames; the highest was in 1809, with the second highest in 1894.

Preston, Crowmarsh Mill, 1927. The mill was closed in 1900 and the tall chimney was demolished in 1905. In 1923 the Benson Mill Syndicate used its water-wheels to generate electricity.

The staff, Preston, Crowmarsh electricity generating station, 1927. Thomas Dearlove is the young boy sitting cross-legged.

'Keep the countryside beautiful': a petrol station and restaurant on the Old London Road midway between Benson and Beggar Bush Hill. It was demolished in 1941 when runways were lengthened at the Benson RAF station.

London Road Inn, Beggar Bush Hill, Benson. Mr C.F. Steventon, an ex-RAF officer, was landlord in the mid-1930s when the top storey was damaged by fire and the inn was converted to a single storey.

The Lamb Inn, between Benson and Ewelme, *c.* 1938. Here, Mr Miners the landlord is standing with his granddaughter. The inn was demolished in 1941 when the airfield runways were extended.

Acknowledgements

In the past twenty-four years I have built up a collection of about five thousand postcards and photographs of the Wallingford area, and a similar number of copies of newspaper cuttings from that excellent local newspaper the *Berks and Oxon Advertiser*. With such a large number to choose from it was difficult to decide what to leave out.

With most of the photographs I have tried to include a newspaper story with the caption and as many names of local people as possible.

There are a number of people who must be thanked for their contributions of photographs, information or encouragement:

Mrs Atkins • Roy Atkins • Tony Crabbe • Mike Gilbey • Malcolm Graham and his excellent staff at the Centre for Oxfordshire Studies • Peter Hoddinott Tony Morris • Olive Robinson • Harold Waite • Marie and Charlie Warwick Wallingford Museum • and Adam and Hayley, my son and daughter, who with great patience guided me through the mysteries of a word processor.

If there is anyone that I have missed out, I apologize; over twenty-four years it is difficult to remember everyone.